TODDLER
*tuesday**

* TRUE TALES FROM THE TODDLER TRENCHES

Library of Congress Cataloging-in-Publication data is available
Identifiers: 978-1-955077-06-4 (Hardback) | 978-1-955077-07-1 (Paperback) | 978-1-955077-08-8 (eBook)

Editing & design by Krista Huber
Illustrations by Shelby Koehler

10 9 8 7 6 5 4 3 2 1
First printing edition 2021

East 26th Publishing
Houston, TX

www.east26thpublishing.com

LEARN MORE:

@toddler_tuesday_books
www.oliveandtate.com

FOR GRAY, WHO MADE ME A MOM
+
FOR GEORGIA, THE OG TODDLER

TODDLER

tuesday ✳

STEPHANIE NICHOLSON

✳ TRUE TALES FROM THE TODDLER TRENCHES

EAST 26TH
PUBLISHING

CONTENTS

DEAR READER

MOM FRIENDS

SEVEN TRUTHS

THE TEMPER TANTRUM

RISE & SHINE

THOUGHTS FROM MY MOM CAR

TARDY

ABC 123

THE ALONE-TIME SNEAK

DEAR PRE-BABY BOOBS

AN OPEN LETTER TO DINNERTIME

DINING OUT

DONT EAT THAT

DOCTOR, DOCTOR

UNSUSPECTING BYSTANDER

FRIENDLY SKIES

INSULTS AND OTHER ONE-LINERS

ZOOM

COOL MOM SEEKS

SECRET'S OUT

POTTY TRAINING

REST STOP

NEVER HAVE I EVER

DUDE'S DAY

THE END

THANK YOU

DEAR READER,

Congratulations! If you're holding this book, you're either one hell of a fun mom or someone in your life thinks you're rocking a fabulous sense of humor. Be sure to go ahead and pat yourself on the back before turning this page because you're going to need both hands to handle the crazy ahead.

Before we begin, allow me to introduce myself:

I'm Stephanie, the creator of a wild little corner of the internet called Olive and Tate. I'm a mom, home renovation dabbler, writer and, dare I say, fun friend. Once a week, I crank up the crazy and host a virtual get-together called #TODDLERTUESDAY. Inspired by my very own offspring, my virtual crew of fellow parents and toddler adjacent cohorts share toddler horror stories straight from the trenches of parenthood.

After years of sharing our stories, I thought it was high time we make things official and save this toddler goodness for posterity's sake. If you were hoping for a *What to Expect When You're Expecting*-style guide to child rearing, I'm afraid you're in the wrong place. Instead, this book is more along the lines of *Sh*t They Should Have Told You: Toddler Years*. Don't say I didn't warn you!

And speaking of warnings...

Everything that you're about to read in this book is true.*

Names and identifying details have been changed in order to maintain toddler anonymity, but the hilarity is real.

My hope is that this book brings you the deep-down belly laughs that might just wake the baby but are *oh-so* worth it.

Welcome to the best of the best/worst of the worst that motherhood has to offer, toddlerhood style.

GODSPEED,

Stephanie

---

* No really, all this shit actually happened. In some places, submissions have been edited for grammar, length and clarity—but never content.

MOM

FRIENDS

I'M HERE TO SAY IT:

THERE IS NO WAY I COULD SURVIVE MOTHERHOOD WITHOUT MY FELLOW TROOPS IN THE MOM TRENCHES.

Individually, we've seen some shit, but if I know one thing, it's this:

No one woman should have to see it all when it comes to Motherhood. It's just too great a burden to bear. Instead we need other wide-eyed, equally shocked and worn down moms who are willing to get in there with us, shoulder some of that truth burden, and wade through.

Are you standing on the motherhood battlefield alone? Don't worry, I got you.

This book was written during a time when it was made clear that a support posse can come in all forms. In this case, it's coming at ya in book form. Every kind of Mom Friend that you could ever want exists right here in those hot little hands of yours. You'll find irreverent, loving, honest, sarcastic, bold and bemused parents in these pages and I am so happy for you to meet them.

And just in case you need my tribe plus a little in-person mom to mom banter,

HERE ARE FIVE TYPES OF MAMAS THAT YOU ABSOLUTELY NEED IN YOUR LIFE (AND WHERE TO FIND THEM):

1.

THE JUSTIFYING MOM

My absolute favorite type of mom friend is the mama who is there to support my less-than-conventional parenting moves. No matter how desperate the situation gets, she's the first to employ a White House-worthy spin on it to make a girl feel better about her stellar motherhood skills.

So the kids had popcorn for dinner? She's quick to point out that popcorn was once a healthy ear of corn so, really, it's not so far off from serving the base of that damn food pyramid.

Your offspring had unlimited screen time for an entire day? No problem! Just think of the hand/eye coordination those kiddos are developing.

The Justifying Mom is always looking out for you, reminding you that you've got this shit and she's got you.

WHERE TO FIND HER: the Chick-fil-A play place.

She'll be scrolling social media while her kids hit the slide because the best dinners are the ones that come with a toy.

2.

THE SAME-STAGE-AS-YOU MOM

There might not be a mom more valuable to stash in your mom arsenal than a mama who has a baby exactly the same age as one of your own.

She's right there in the trenches with you, unjaded and worrying about the same things that you are.

Who else could you possibly text "should her poop be neon orange?" (complete with photo evidence) without a preemptive warning?

If it weren't for my Same-Stage Mamas, I probably would have expected my firstborn to crawl at four months and held off on solids until he had a tooth.

WHERE TO FIND HER: story hour at the library.

It's free, segregated by age, and you can gauge her level of chill by her enthusiasm over the chicken dance.

3.

THE BEEN-THERE-DONE-THAT MOM

She's seen it all, baby. She'll be the first to remind you that "were you breastfed or formula fed?" will not be on your child's college applications (and that he won't take that pacifier with him when he goes).

The memories of sleepless nights are a bit hazier for her, but her perspective on what really matters is invaluable. When you feel like teething will never end, she'll be the one to point out that braces are just around the corner and, unlike teething, braces ain't free.

This mama will inspire you to appreciate your littles when they're little, but remind you not to sweat the small stuff because you'll be onto the next stage before you know it.

WHERE TO FIND HER: the school volunteer committee you were roped into joining.

She'll be one of the head honchos because she's been around a while. And, since you're friends, she won't stick you with clean up duty.

4.

THE SYMPATHIZING MOM

She's the first to pour you a cup of coffee when you find out your kid is the biter in class, during day three of potty training or after that time you had to drag your screaming preschooler out of a children's theatre show about balloons.

Bless her, the Sympathizing Mom never asks why, never suggests you read that latest parenting book on the "spirited child" and never, ever starts a sentence with "Well, have you tried...?"

She's calm and steady, ready to remind you that you will survive this motherhood thing, even if just barely.

WHERE TO FIND HER: the pediatrician's office.

You'll bond over your respective baby ear infections and she'll know the best remedy to help your little sicky sleep (and the best wine you can grab at CVS to help *you* sleep).

5.

THE DOWN-FOR-WHATEVER MOM

Just got a call from your S.O. that they'll be working late?

This mama is your go-to girl for a last minute Happy Meal and wine playdate dinner.

She is flexible, doesn't take her schedule too seriously and you never clean your house for her.

She's the one who won't roll her eyes when you tell her you just can't handle another snow day off from school and she always knows which playground is closest to a Starbucks.

Basically, she's down to do whatever it takes to make it through the day.

Bonus: she has never once made a kid-friendly craft from Pinterest.

WHERE TO FIND HER: at the playground, sitting on a bench while her kids are in shouting distance.

She definitely won't be hovering near the slide to make sure they stick the landing.

WHATEVER TYPE OF MOM FRIEND YOU NEED,
WE'VE GOT YOU COVERED.

SHE'S RIGHT HERE, IN THIS BOOK, GATHERED AROUND YOU TO
MAKE YOU LAUGH, SHOW YOU THE ROPES AND REMIND YOU THAT
IT COULD ALWAYS (AND I DO MEAN ALWAYS) BE WORSE.

MEET MY VERY EXTENDED, VERY HONEST AND VERY EXPERIENCED
COHORTS THAT ARE ABOUT TO BESTOW UPON YOU THEIR
EXPERIENCES BATTLING THE TRUEST TERRORS KNOWN TO MAN:

Toddlers

SEVEN

TRUTHS

BUT FIRST,
SOME GROUND RULES:

Toddlers are a unique species of their own. They come complete with their own set of rules, commandments, and a somewhat flighty moral code.

As it turns out, mothering a toddler is not for the faint of heart. One minute I'm Mary Poppins and the next minute I'm the chick from Game of Thrones. Frankly, neither are a good look for me.

I've put together a little list of commands that I wish I had known before my son's second birthday. My hope is that these truths will provide you with a bit of a road map to Toddler Land, just in case you are staring into the abyss of an empty bag of Goldfish with hours to go until nap time.

1. CLEANING IS FOR FOOLS.

No matter how hard you try to contain the filth, your toddler will follow behind you emptying cabinets, slinging a yogurt pouch onto the baseboards[1], spilling juice from a spill-proof cup, and spitting half-chewed Strawberry Frosted Mini Wheats onto your white sheets.[2]

You'll do your best to keep up, but you are no match for the space destroying powers of a toddler.

It's best to go ahead and resign yourself to a life of living in a house that looks like the "before" shot of a Fixer Upper episode.

2. SHOES ARE MYSTERIOUS.

My son currently owns two pairs of the same shoe in two different colors. On certain days, he prefers his blue shoes and on the other days, he's all about the orange pair.

But you wanna know a secret? He likes to hide the pair he wants to wear and then request them. Yeah, he's fun like that. If I had a cup of coffee for every minute I spent searching for one orange shoe, I would never be tired again.

3. NUGGETS ARE THEIR OWN NUTRITIONAL PYRAMID SCHEME.

Let's face it, hell hath no fury like a toddler who just ran out of chicken nuggets. Before I had my son, I thought *Oh, I'll only do nuggets occasionally—you know, in between organic spinach and cauliflower rice.*

Now I buy chicken nuggets in catering trays so that they are always in my refrigerator.

My, how the mighty have fallen.

---

1   FYI, that one took straight bleach to remove.
2   Another FYI, the pink "strawberry" color stains.

4. YOU WILL ENGAGE IN SHADY BEHAVIOR.

Listen, I know you're a good person.

So am I, for the most part.

But here's the rub: parenting a toddler may cause you to lie, cheat, and steal with the skill of a seasoned con man.

Don't believe me?

Try opening a bag of chips within earshot of a toddler.

She'll come running, and before she can get her crazy little hands near you, you'll be lying to her face in no time flat.

You'll make up stories about everything from bedtime to broccoli, and you'll sell them with such enthusiasm you may just start to believe them yourselves.

5. BODILY FLUIDS ARE MEANT TO BE SHARED.

I'm fairly certain that I've never been exposed to so many bodily fluids on a regular basis in my life. And not just those of the diaper variety.

Boogers, snot, slobber, spit, whatever the black stuff under his nails is—it's all out there, all the time.

And I'm the one who either gets showered in it, or has to clean it up, or both.

6. COLORS ARE IMPORTANT.

Just as a warning, you should know that you will never, ever choose the right color sippy cup before you fill it with milk. Ever.

If by some miracle, you do choose correctly, I can promise you that you won't be able to find a lid that matches that cup.

And God help you if you need to pick out a set of toddler cutlery.

7. CHILDPROOFING IS LAUGHABLE.

Installing baby gates, toilet locks, or those fancy cabinet magnet brackets is the equivalent to throwing down the toddler gauntlet.

Your toddler will see your efforts to keep him safe as a challenge to prove how ineffective those pricey little gadgets really are.

And he will do so with frightening speed and efficiency.

I've never seen my toddler concentrate on something as hard as he concentrates on getting that toilet lid open so he can throw his bath toys right down the hatch.

If any of this sounds familiar to you, know that I am with you in solidarity and in the bonds of motherhood.

But while this is a scared space, full of respect and love, you should know one thing: if you thought it couldn't possibly get any more gross, louder or more poop-covered than in your own home, sit back and relax, baby...

The stories in this book are about to rock your world.

THE

TEMPER TANTRUM

AS WE BEGIN OUR JOURNEY...

into the tales of toddlerhood survival, it feels only natural to start on comfortable territory.

Temper Tantrum. Throwing A Fit. Showing Out. Acting A Fool.

Whatever you wanna call it, nothing can bring a parent to their knees quite like a public toddler throw down.

In that moment when the aisles are closing in and the screams are echoing, just remember this: there is, without a doubt, another mom across the store thinking, "Keep it up! You're a tough mom bitch who has handled much worse. Don't let that tiny tyrant get the best of you."

Don't believe me?

I have the war stories to prove it.

"

Today at church, my three-year-old had to go to the bathroom (#2). Of course, the bathroom was crowded but we got her into a stall and settled. I was standing by, holding the stall door closed, when she yelled, "A big one is coming! Jesus is going to LOVE it!"

I was equal parts embarrassed, amused and grossed out by her bringing Jesus into the situation and whisper-yelled at her to *hurry up* through the door, hoping to end our misery ASAP.

But then.

When none of the strangers in the bathroom praised her for going #2 (and a big #2 at that)...

The temper tantrum ensued.

She actually had a temper tantrum on the toilet over not being praised for her big, Jesus-pleasing #2.

"

@kateallisonspencer

"

My then two-year-old spilled an entire juice box on her dress at lunch.

She took her own dress off and then lost her shit that her "boobies would be cold."

"

Tampon-sicle

MY SON SOBBED BECAUSE I WOULDN'T LET HIM EAT
A TAMPON THAT HE THOUGHT WAS A POPSICLE.

@amronn4

> I didn't zip up my two-year-old's coat to the appropriate spot she wanted.
>
> Every spot I tried was wrong.
>
> Three coat changes later, we ended up with a Velcro one just so we could get the F out the door 20 minutes later.

@kmombert

Mom kidnapper

MY SON THREW A FIT DURING CHURCH SO OUT WE WENT INTO THE HALLWAY.

HE THEN LOST IT AGAIN WHEN I WOULDN'T GO BACK INTO THE SERVICE
BECAUSE, GO FIGURE, HE WAS STILL SCREAMING.

AFTER THINGS CONTINUED TO ESCALATE IN THE HALL, AND WITH THE
SANCTUARY CLEARLY NOT AN OPTION, I TOOK HIM TO THE CAR, HOPING THE
PARKING LOT SCREAMS WOULDN'T CARRY INTO THE BUILDING.

WE FINALLY MADE IT TO THE CAR AND I ATTEMPTED TO STRAP HIM INTO HIS
CARSEAT, STILL MID TANTRUM, BUT HE WASN'T HAVING IT.

HE FOUGHT ME SO HARD, SCREAMING BLOODY MURDER AND
CREATING SUCH A SCENE THAT AN ACTUAL SHERIFF CAME OVER TO SEE
WHAT WAS GOING ON.

@josephinennAthall

RISE &

SHINE

IT'S BEEN SCIENTIFICALLY PROVEN[1] THAT WE MOMS DO THIS CUTE LITTLE THING CALLED "NIGHTTIME REBELLION"[2] IN WHICH WE STAY UP WAY TOO LATE JUST TO SOAK IN THAT DELICIOUSLY QUIET ALONE-TIME FEELING.

IT ALL FEELS SO SOOTHING AND CUP-FILLING WHEN WE FINALLY SNEAK INTO BED, FINGERS CROSSED THAT TONIGHT WILL BE THE NIGHT WE GET THOSE RECOMMENDED 8 HOURS.

And then...

---

1   I mean, I'm sure it has been, but I didn't actually research this, so don't quote me.
2   As it turns out, this *has* been researched and it's aptly called "Revenge Bedtime Procrastination."

Dixie cup surprise

"Mom look what I found!"

I open my eyes to see my son holding a Dixie cup. At this point his hand is over the top.

As I awaken and say, "What?" he releases his hand, pointing the cup at me.

What he "found" was a mouse.

It leapt from the cup onto my face and down my pajama top. I have never screamed so loud in my life!

Meanwhile, my son is devastated because I lost his new pet.

@gram2380

Recently, my three-year-old came into our room to tell us about
the man who reads her books in the middle of the night.

"He's so funny, mommy! He look like my PawPaw! Mommy, tell him to come back!"

PawPaw has passed.

Needless to say, it happened once...
then it happened twice...
and now we sleep with our lights on.

@lindseyreganthorne

Frying pan wake-up

I'M A LOT PREGNANT WITH BABY #2. HUBBY IS DEPLOYED.

TODDLER IS WATCHING TANGLED.

I TAKE ADVANTAGE OF THE QUIET MOMENT AND
TRY TO GET IN A NAP ON THE COUCH.

AT THIS MOMENT, TODDLER DECIDED TO RE-ENACT THE FRYING PAN SCENE
WITH HER METAL TOY PAN FROM IKEA...ON MY SLEEPING HEAD.

@coughlin-partyof5

"

I must have dozed off and the next thing I know, my two-year-old
squatted on my face while taking a poop in her diaper.

It smelled awful.

Like, literally on my face, one leg on each side of my head
and diaper right smack in the middle of my face.

"

@mdsa_dy

Warm crevices

OUR DAUGHTER LIKES TO SNEAK INTO OUR BED AT NIGHT. HER FEET AND TOES GET COLD, SO SHE WEDGES THEM UNDER OUR BODIES, INTO CREVICES—WHEREEVER SHE CAN FIND WARMTH.

TURNS OUT THAT A VERY WARM PLACE IS INSIDE MY UNDERPANTS, BETWEEN MY CHEEKS! I FELT HER TINY TOES WIGGLING TO FIND THEIR WAY, WOKE UP ABRUPTLY AND SAID ABSOLUTELY NOT.

@rubysoho44

THOUGHTS
MOM

FROM MY CAR

ONCE, IN A LIFE LIVED LONG AGO,

THERE WAS A TIME WHEN GRABBING MY TEENY
TINY PURSE, PRANCING OUT OF THE HOUSE AND HOPPING
INTO MY MID-SIZED VEHICLE WAS SECOND NATURE.

MY CAR WAS A MEANS TO GET ME TO AND FRO—FROM MANICURES
TO COCKTAILS, AND CERTAINLY NOT AN EXPERIENCE UNTO ITSELF.

AND NOW?

NOW THINGS ARE JUST SLIGHTLY DIFFERENT...
AND SMELL A LOT WORSE.

Thoughts I have when I'm in my car:

WHAT IS THAT SMELL?

I HAVE GOT TO REMEMBER TO CRACK THE WINDOWS
AT NIGHT SO THIS THING CAN AIR OUT.

WHEN WILL THIS KID LEARN TO BUCKLE HIMSELF IN?

I SHOULD REALLY START CARRYING FULL SIZED TRASH BAGS IN THIS CAR.

WHY ARE ALL OF MY CUP HOLDERS ALWAYS FULL?

I SHOULD GET MORE CUP HOLDERS.

CAN YOU BUY CUP HOLDERS FOR CARS? I WONDER IF STROLLER
CUP HOLDERS WILL CLIP ON SOMEWHERE.

NO, WE CANNOT LISTEN TO DISNEY RADIO.

I CAN NEVER FIND A PEN WHEN I NEED ONE.

I WONDER IF THE BANK WILL ACCEPT A CHECK WRITTEN IN CRAYON...

I SHOULD PROBABLY THROW AWAY YESTERDAY'S CHICK-FIL-A
TRASH BEFORE WE DRIVE THROUGH AGAIN TODAY.

MAYBE THAT SMELL IS A CHICKEN NUGGET LOST
UNDER THE SEATS SOMEWHERE.

WHY IS MY STEERING WHEEL STICKY?

EVERY PLACE ON EARTH SHOULD HAVE A DRIVE-THROUGH. I WILL DRIVE
ACROSS TOWN TO THE DRY CLEANER WITH A DRIVE-THROUGH AND NOT THINK
TWICE ABOUT IT. IF I OPENED A BUSINESS, IT WOULD DEFINITELY HAVE A
DRIVE-THROUGH.

GOD, THAT COUNTING APP IS ANNOYING.

I WONDER WHEN KIDS START WEARING HEADPHONES?

LISTEN TO HIM COUNTING! HE'S SOOOOO SMART!

THE CHICK-FIL-A DRIVE-THROUGH GIRL JUST CALLED ME BY NAME.
AT LEAST SHE KNOWS TO DOUBLE DOWN ON THE POLYNESIAN SAUCE.

I WILL THROW THAT IPAD OUT THE WINDOW IF HE DOESN'T
START PLAYING ANOTHER DAMN APP.

I WONDER IF I CAN GET AWAY WITH DRIVING ALL THE WAY HOME
BEFORE HE STARTS SCREAMING FOR CHICKEN NUGGETS.

BITES CHICKEN NUGGETS INTO 100 PIECES AND HANDS THEM BACK

WAIT, DOES HE HAVE STICKERS?

NO. NO STICKERS ON MY WINDOWS.

DO WE OWN GOO GONE?

OH HEY, DAD IN THE MINIVAN, I SEE YOU ROCKING THAT KID
WAGON AND I'M JEALOUS OF YOUR DVD PLAYER.

SO MANY RED LIGHTS, SO FEW MINUTES UNTIL NAP TIME.

I THINK MY NEXT CAR NEEDS WI-FI SO WE CAN STREAM
ANYTHING OTHER THAN THE COUNTING APP.

I WONDER IF THIS CHICKEN NUGGET-COVERED SALAD IS
REALLY HEALTHY. LIKE, COULD I JUST ORDER A #1 COMBO INSTEAD?

OH, NO SIR! DON'T YOU EVEN THINK ABOUT FALLING ASLEEP IN THIS CAR!

SINGS AT THE TOP OF MY LUNGS TO PREVENT A CAR NAP

ALMOST HOME, ALMOST HOME, ALMOST HOME.

PLEASE TRANSFER, PLEASE TRANSFER, PLEASE TRANSFER.

OK, BUT SERIOUSLY, WHAT IS THAT SMELL?

TARDY

CLOSE YOUR EYES, SIT BACK, RELAX...

and let your mind wander to a place long, long ago.

It's a happy place. A slow place. A place of hot coffee, tiny purses and lazy mornings.

It's a place of shaving your legs, lounging in a bath and long, drawn out brunches.

In this place, you are organized, presentable and never, ever late. You leave your house with ease, have full control of your radio, and arrive to your destination refreshed.

Do you remember this place?

Yeah, me either.

Instead, we were recently late because my daughter managed to lock herself *and* our Goldendoodle inside of the dog's crate.

Together. In a dog crate.

My youngest had a blowout on the way to daycare.

I knew because my oldest asked,
"Where did brother get chocolate!?"

I looked back and it was ON HIS FACE.

Definitely not chocolate.

Pantry brushing

WE COULDN'T LEAVE THE HOUSE THIS MORNING BECAUSE MY
TWO-YEAR-OLD REFUSED TO LEAVE THE PANTRY.

SHE SHUT HERSELF IN SO SHE COULD BRUSH HER TEETH "ALL BY
MYSELF"...IN THE PANTRY.

IT TOOK A GOOD FIFTEEN MINUTES TO GET HER OUT.

The victimizer in this story is not my own children
...but in fact, me.

I once acted like I had lice at daycare right after my
mom walked out so that they would run out to the
parking lot and have her come back in to wait with
me until they could check my head.

It worked, and surprise, surprise, no lice was found!

@brookenhevt

My goddaughter apparently threw her mom's car keys
in the trash one evening when her mom wasn't looking.

Fast forward to the next day....which was garbage day...

BEFORE WE COULD LEAVE THE HOUSE, WE HAD TO
WAIT FOR MY TWO-YEAR-OLD'S ERECTION TO GO AWAY.

HIM CRYING

"MY PENIS IS BIGGGGGGG! I WANT IT WHITTTLLLLLEEEE!"

ABC

123

HAVE YOU EVER WONDERED...

what exactly your toddler talks about at preschool all day?

With their propensity to mix up important narrative details while simultaniously losing all grasp of the English language and ignoring formerly-established boundaries, it's possible that literally anything could come out of their mouths at any time.

All I can say is:

God bless teachers.

Star Wars play

"

When my daughter was three she told her daycare teacher that her daddy has
Star Wars underwear and that he and I "dress like Star Wars and play."

It definitely came off to the teacher as something sexual but I swear I have a
Leia costume and my husband has a Storm Trooper costume for Halloween ONLY.

"

@kriskel

Bible spit balls

MY OLDEST DAUGHTER CHECKED OUT
"THE CHILDREN'S BIBLE" FROM HER SCHOOL LIBRARY.

MY YOUNGEST DAUGHTER FOUND SAID BOOK, TORE PAGES OUT, CRUMBLED TINY
SPIT BALLS OUT OF THE PAGES AND SHOVED
EIGHT OF THEM UP HER TINY LITTLE NOSE.

WE HAD TO TAKE HER TO THE ER BECAUSE I COULDN'T REACH THEM
ALL WITH TWEEZERS.

I'M SURE THE SCHOOL LIBRARIAN WILL NEVER FORGET US.

@kristen_chicago

Robot boobies

> My daughter was on her class Zoom meeting.
>
> The lesson that day was a step-by-step guide
> on how to draw a robot.
>
> She got bored, took a little creative license and announced
> to the entire class, "Look everybody! My robot has boobies!"
>
> She had, in fact, given her robot some lovely DD's

@cait5toff

Jell-O shots

"

When my son was three, his preschool teacher asked me to stay a few minutes after class for a quick meeting.

She proceeded to tell me that my child told her that I took him to a party where he got to have JELL-O shots.

I was completely embarrassed while I explained that we had attended a friend's Doc McStuffins themed birthday party where they served plastic syringes filled with red (alcohol free!) JELL-O.

"

@hsmamaof2

Dinner droppings

MY SON IS ALMOST THREE AND WENT POTTY BEFORE DINER BUT
DIDN'T WANT TO PUT HIS PANTS AND UNDERWEAR BACK ON.

HUSBAND TOLD HIM JOKINGLY,
"DON'T DROP ANY DINNER ON YOUR PENIS!"

THOUGHT THAT WAS THE END OF THAT.

THE NEXT MORNING, MY SON RUNS INTO HIS CLASSROOM,
GIVES HIS TEACHER A BIG HUG, AND EXCITEDLY TELLS HER,
"I DIDN'T GET ANY DINNER ON MY PENIS LAST NIGHT!"

I JUST STOOD THERE SPEECHLESS.

@svtlein36

THE
TIME

ALONE
SNEAK

THE OLDER I GET, AND
THE LESS TIME I HAVE TO MYSELF,

the more it becomes clear to me that I am an introvert.

I know it seems odd that I would have so little self-awareness, and that I am just now (in my thirties) realizing where I stand on the personality charts. But, to be fair, I'm really outgoing in social settings.

I love public speaking, become more animated and sociable when I'm nervous, and honestly get a kick out of making small talk.

But once the crowds have parted, the last drop has been poured and the night is over, I find myself so incredibly drained that my body feels like I've just run a marathon. I simply cannot function until I have some time alone, in silence, to get myself together.

Before motherhood, I could always count on driving in the car alone to gather myself. I would use my commute to ditch the work stress and gear myself up for dinner, the weekend, or even one-on-one time with my husband.

But now?

Now, I am never alone.

Ever.

In the hunt for a moment of solitude, I've picked up some really bad habits that I don't think are doing me any favors—namely, staying up really late and watching TV.

I know I should go to bed, that the baby will be up soon, that I function better with a good night's sleep, but the alone time is just so...delicious.

I lay there sipping wine from what is most likely a plastic cup, watching a rerun of The Big Bang Theory that I can quote and soak in the silence. No one needs me, a snack, a meal, a bill paid, a favor, a hug or a band aid.

Thinking about my late-night hideaway got my wheels turning about the other ways that I sneak alone time, and as it turns out, some of them are down right shameful.

GET FOOD POISONING

I got a fun little case of food poisoning from the local Mexican joint up the street, and I can assure you that my husband did not mind spending time with the baby outside of the house just to be away from all of the vomiting.

SLEEP IN THE GUEST ROOM BECAUSE "THE DOG IS SNORING"

She does snore. Sometimes.
So does my husband. Sometimes.

But sometimes I just hide in the guest room because I can sleep
in the middle of the bed and not be touched by anyone else for an entire night.

FOLD LAUNDRY

I pile up the laundry on the living room sofa, secure the baby in his playroom where I can see him, and turn on an MTV marathon of Teen Mom. Nothing accompanies a session of folding laundry like the mind-numbing bliss that is a Teen Mom repeat.

Sometimes, my mind gets so numb that I forget to fold the laundry.

CLEAN OUT THE CAR

Sometimes when I stop to fill up for gas, I take an extra long time cleaning out the loose odds and ends from my vehicle and tossing them in the trash.

I'm talking one fry at a time, as many trips to the trash can as possible, all in blissful silence while the baby waits patiently for me in his car seat.

GO TO THE DOCTOR

Listen, we all know when you go to the doctor for a non-emergency reason, you are going to wait forever. The last time I hit the OB/GYN for an annual visit, I booked a babysitter for four solid hours and treated that doctor's appointment like a spa visit.

With a hot coffee, a fresh magazine and some solid WiFi, I was happy to sit alone in a paper gown for as long as they needed me to wait.

The dentist or eye doctor will also do in a pinch.

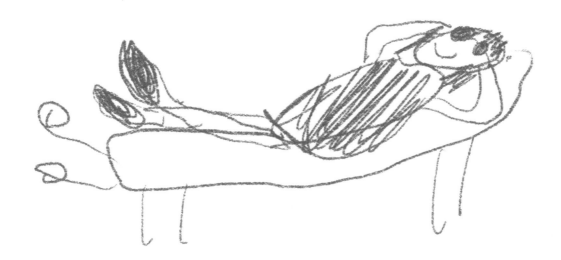

DEAR PRE-

BABY BOOBS,

I'M SO SORRY THAT I EVER

wished for you to be bigger, that I never appreciated your ability to hold yourself up in a strapless dress or be supported by a thin tube top.

You were always there for me, happily pointing in the same direction and easily corralled by a cheap bra from the Juniors' section of Target.

I'm sorry that I never paid you more respect, bought you the good bras from Nordstrom, had you professionally measured or bragged about you more. Forgive me; I was young and naive.

I thought I spared you. You couldn't feed the baby and I didn't resent you. Instead, I celebrated the prospect of you bouncing back to your old selves and me being able to drink all of the wine.

I'm sorry for what happened to you.

The doctor told me that I gained just the right amount of weight, but you bore the brunt of the pregnancy flux. My pre-pregnancy jeans can stretch to manage the load that is my hips but those pre-pregnancy bras are no match for you.

I miss you.

Will you come back?

I promise to buy you nice things; to treat you with kindness and the respect you deserve.

I'll be here waiting, silky backless top in hand. You know where to find me.

Please come back.

I love you.

> After the birth of my third kid, my middle child was watching me nurse our newborn.
>
> He asked me what was on my chest, and then, before waiting for me to answer, he said, "Meatballs? You have meatballs on your chest?"
>
> I responded, "No, these are called nipples. And I feed the baby my milk this way."
>
> The next day, in front of his new preschool teacher he says, "My mom's milk comes out of her meatballs. It's amazing."

@Flbferg

Baby booty

WHILE I WAS PREGNANT WITH MY THIRD DAUGHTER, MY OLDER TWO GIRLS
WOULD ALWAYS COMMENT ON HOW BIG MY BELLY WAS GETTING.

THEY KNEW THERE WAS A BABY GROWING INSIDE AND WERE
EXCITED TO MEET HER!

ONE MORNING WHILE I WAS GETTING DRESSED, MY OLDEST
DAUGHTER ASKED ME IF I HAD A SECOND BABY GROWING IN MY BUTT
BECAUSE MY BUTT WAS GETTING AS BIG AS MY BELLY.

Jump, mommy!

YOU COULD SAY I'M 'BLESSED' IN THE CHEST DEPARTMENT.
ALSO, THEY ARE MUCH LARGER THAN NORMAL BECAUSE I'M
NURSING OUR THIRD CHILD.

SHORTLY AFTER I HAD OUR THIRD BABY, I WAS GETTING DRESSED IN MY
BEDROOM WHEN MY FOUR-YEAR-OLD KINDLY BARGED IN, CHATTERING AWAY.

SHE SUDDENLY STOPPED TALKING...GLUED HER EYEBALLS TO MY CHEST
(I HAD NO BRA OR SHIRT ON AT THIS POINT), AND POINT BLANK ASKED
IF I COULD JUMP FOR HER.

NO. NO, CHILD I WILL NOT JUMP FOR YOU.

@mikhailaanheim

> My toddler enjoys being naked (as most do).
>
> One evening as she sat there in her birthday suit,
> I said, "Oh! Can mommy be naked, too?"
>
> Her response was, "No, mommy. I don't like your body."

@dani_michexoxo

AN OPEN LETTER TO DINNERTIME

DEAR DINNERTIME,

DON'T TAKE THIS THE WRONG WAY, BUT I LEGITIMATELY LOATHE YOU.

I GET IT, TRUST ME, I DO. SHARED DINNER IS IMPORTANT FOR THE STABILITY OF MY FAMILY UNIT, INSTILS CONFIDENCE IN MY OFFSPRING, SHOWS OFF MY DOMESTIC PROWESS AND ALL THAT.

BUT HONESTLY, I JUST CAN'T WITH YOU ANYMORE.

SO TONIGHT, WHILE MY FAMILY WAS SLOWLY, BUT SURELY, REFUSING TO EAT EVERY BITE OF THE MEAL I LOVINGLY SLAVED OVER, I CAME UP WITH A LIST OF REASONS WHY YOU SUCK SO HARD.

SO, WITHOUT FURTHER ADO, HERE ARE THE TOP FOUR REASONS DINNERTIME CAN GO EFF ITSELF:

THE TIME

How is it that Dinner shows up at the worst part of our day, every day?

Right smack in the middle of the newborn's Witching Hour and my pre-schooler's nightly meltdown over his socks being too tight, Dinner presents itself in the form of an empty fridge and a hungry family.

And just for the record, even if the fridge wasn't empty, there would still be "nothing to eat."

I nightly praise the Gods Of All Things Processed for microwavable mac + cheese cups and yogurt in a tube.

THE FORETHOUGHT

Somehow, while wearing a screaming baby and finding the Everest episode of Paw Patrol on the DVR, I'm supposed to scheme up, organize and prep a beautiful meal, all while fighting the urge to lie down and mainline boxed wine.

Oh, wait.

Was I supposed to have taken my two wild beasts to the actual grocery store with a list and a prayer in order to pull this whole Dinner thing off?

Thanks, but no thanks.

THE PROCESS

Let me be clear here, it's not just the actual meal prep that fuels my hate fire.

It's the process of dragging everyone to the table, ideally with pants on, requesting that everyone use their napkin and that no one wipe their boogers on anyone else that really wears me down.

I mean, how many times can one woman say, "We don't put our feet on the table!" before losing her mind?

Hint: the answer is infinity.

THE AFTERMATH

And then.

Then, after all of that effort and Pinteresting, Dinner is over in two minutes flat.

Over and barely consumed and discarded for yours truly to clean up.

So many dishes, so little cares to give. The only silver lining to the endless cycle that is kitchen clean up is that everyone manages to vanish the second the dishes hit the sink... which means mama can scrape plates in peace.

And honestly, with all of the dishwasher steam and scented dish soap bubbles, I can close my eyes and almost feel the spa vibes.

Almost.

It's no wonder my three-year-old can order our family dinner on the Dominos app unassisted.

Sincerely,
The Mom Who Served Lunchables[1] for Dinner (Again)

---

1   Lunchables are life.

DINING

ALTERNATE TITLE: JUST THROW YOUR

OUT
MONEY STRAIGHT INTO THE TRASH

AH, RESTAURANTS.

I used to truly love dining out.

I mean, who wouldn't?

Restaurants are full of meals cooked by other people, dishes washed by anyone but you and a person paid to fetch that Kraft Mac & Cheese you could have easily made at home.

And then, I had toddler.

My adoration for a non-home cooked mealtime experience slowly waned as I realized all of the complexities that come with feeding a toddler in public. There was a time when I thought we could power through and learn to love a dinner out with little kids in tow. That was only until the tampon incident put an end to it all.

At a very popular and crowded local burger spot, my toddler daughter took advantage of a single second's walk past my open purse on her way to the bathroom with her dad.

She reacher her tiny hand in, pulled out a tampon, slipped her other hand away from my husband's grasp and ran through the restaurant waving said tampon above her head.

Turns out, she thought it was candy. Her victory lap was accompanied by her shouting, "I want more candy! I want more candy JUST LIKE DIS ONE!"

I'm sure you can imagine the game of catch that ensued between my husband and daughter. We managed to draw every single eye in the building as she darted through tables and bumped into chairs with her tiny tampon-wielding hand.

We haven't been back to that burger joint since.

There will be insects...

"

We were eating at a restaurant when our son was still in the crawling phase.

He made a dash for it and when we managed to wrangle him back, he had a cockroach in his mouth.

"

There will be pee...

> A couple of years ago we took our two girls to Chick-fil-A, like we did weekly.
>
> The girls were playing in the play place and my youngest comes out with pee on her pants. My oldest tells me she peed at the top of the play place.
>
> I'm thinking, "You've got to be kidding me."
>
> So, I grabbed some paper towels and climbed all the way to the top. Cleaned it. Came down.
>
> Then I go to check my youngest's diaper. It was completely dry.
>
> It seems my youngest crawled through a pee puddle that belonged to someone else at the top of the slide...

@gabe_ldridge

There will be poop...

WITH OUR FIRST KID (WE'VE LEARNED AFTER THIS), WE WENT OUT TO A REALLY NICE DINNER FOR MOTHER'S DAY WITH MY AUNT AND GRANDMOTHER.

I DIDN'T BRING IN THE HUGE DIAPER BAG—JUST ONE DIAPER AND THE WIPES.

KID DECIDES TO GO POOP. AND IT'S UP HIS BACK. AND HE'S BIG.
LIKE, ONE YEAR OLD AND 30LBS BIG.

MY HUSBAND SAID HE WOULD CHANGE HIS DIAPER.
THE MEN'S BATHROOM IS ALL FANCY WHITE MARBLE AND GOLD AND NICE, BUT NO CHANGING TABLE. HUSBAND TRIES TO CALL ME BUT I DON'T ANSWER. HE WALKS BACK THROUGH THE RESTAURANT WITH OUR KID IN JUST A DIAPER.

HE LOOKED AT ME AND SAID, "WE HAVE TO LEAVE NOW."

APPARENTLY, HE DID HIS BEST, BUT MANAGED TO GET POOP ON EVERYTHING AND EVERYWHERE WITHOUT A CHANGING TABLE. HE USED THE ENTIRE PACK OF WIPES AND OUR KIDS CLOTHES TO TRY TO CLEAN IT ALL UP BUT IT WASN'T ENOUGH. EVERYTHING WAS COVERED.

HE NEVER CHANGED A DIRTY DIAPER AGAIN.

@davismeade

There will be vomit...

MY TWO-YEAR-OLD SON WAS THROWING A FIT ABOUT
EATING HIS DINNER AT A RESTAURANT AND SOMEHOW
ENDED UP THROWING UP ALL OVER THE BOOTH...AND MY AUNT.

LUCKILY NONE OF IT ENDED UP ON THE TABLE OR ANYONE'S FOOD.

THE BEST PART OF IT ALL, THOUGH, WAS WHEN I TOOK
HIM TO THE BATHROOM TO CLEAN HIM UP.

HE SAID, "HAPPY BIRTHDAY MOMMY!" IN THE CUTEST,
SWEETEST VOICE. IT WAS NOT MY BIRTHDAY.

@k.wndson

There will be body parts...

> My husband took my son to the restroom
> while we were out to eat and, upon their return,
> my son announced to the restaurant:
> "DADDY HAS A BIG PENIS, MOM!"
>
> I still crack up out loud when I think about it.

@ashleynewtt

DON'T

EAT THAT

WHILE THEY CERTAINLY AREN'T EATING ANY DINNER OF MINE,

it does seem that toddlers have a knack for putting things in their mouths that aren't supposed to be there.

Or worse, putting their mouths in places they shouldn't.

I wondered if it was just my offspring who have an appetite for anything gag-inducing, but our collective gaggle of moms quickly assured me that "disgusting" is the universal toddler language.

And now, a poll—

What's worse: Fishing a foreign object out of your toddler's mouth or pulling their little tongue off of a foreign object?

Not sure where you stand?

Let's do a little experiment to find out.[1]

---

1   Shockingly, the following list contains actual submissions from real moms and real toddler experiences.

HOSPITAL WINDOW & WALL RAILING
HUSBAND'S USED DEODORANT
TODDLER'S OWN SHOE, FRESH FROM A TRIP TO A REST STOP
PASSENGER DOOR OF THE FAMILY SUV
BIRD SHIT ON SIDEWALK
TOILET HANDLE AT THE PEDIATRICIAN'S OFFICE
ATLANTIC CITY STAIRWAY HAND RAILS
THE CHICK INCUBATOR AT THE COUNTY FAIR
THE PUBLIC PARK PLAYGROUND TRASH CAN
THE WATER OUT OF A LIVESTOCK BUCKET
EVERY SHOPPING CART FROM EVERY RETAILER POSSIBLE
TOILET BRUSH, DRIPPING WET FROM TOILET
SUBWAY HANDLES/RAILS
M&M OFF THE FLOOR OF GRANDMA'S NURSING HOME
DAD'S USED JOCKSTRAP
THEIR OWN DIARRHEA
A TUBE OF BUTT PASTE
PETRIFIED CAT POOP
STAGNANT RAIN WATER FROM THE BACK OF A TRICYCLE
AIRPLANE WINDOW

WAS LICKED
BY A TODDLER

DOG FOOD
DEAD ROACH (ANTENNA END OUT)
DOG'S SHORT, DOCKED TAIL
DEER POOP
A TOOTH FOUND ON THE FLOOR OF A DINER
USED TAMPON APPLICATOR
FOUND, PRE-CHEWED GUM
DIVA CUP (CLEAN, BUT PREVIOUSLY USED)
BLOODY PUPPY TOOTH
EARTH WORM
ROGUE ACRYLIC NAIL FROM THE PARK
THEIR OWN SHIT
A FOUND CHEESE CRACKER COVERED IN ANTS
A LIVE SNAIL
TWO SEQUINS STRAIGHT OFF OF MIL'S ENSEMBLE
PIECE OF TRIMMED SHEEP HOOF
CIGARETTE BUTT
A PACIFIER STRAIGHT OUT OF THE TOILET
A DRIED UP, DEAD FROG
TOILET NIGHTLIGHT

WAS RETRIEVED
FROM A
TODDLER'S MOUTH

STILL NOT SURE?

LET ME HELP YOU OUT.

ANSWER: *We lose.*

DOCTOR,

DOCTOR

WANNA KNOW A SECRET?

Once, long ago, my first born toddler launched himself off of our bed and onto the carpeted floor below.

When I rushed to pick him up, his face was red and starting to swell. I just knew something terrible had happened thanks to the angry look of his little forehead.

I did what any rational human would do upon seeing a raw, red toddler mug and ran straight to the local children's emergency room.

I mean, hello! Foreheads are important!

They house our brains and sometimes our poorly thought out bangs and therefore foreheads must be attended to professionally, you know?

After hours in the emergency room, we were seen by a no-nonsense doctor whose face I'll never forget.

He stared deep into my panicked eyes and asked me if my bed happened to be taller than an average bed.

When I confirmed that our bed is not, in fact, a few stories high, he then asked if I knew what covered our floors.

Yes, of course, carpet covered our floors! Thick carpet to keep us warm.....

He sighed, got up off of his doctor stool and asked us to kindly leave so that he could attend to actual sick children.

I was bewildered. Surly he had not seen this child's red, bumpy forehead! I mean, this tiny kid fell. off. a. bed.

As Dr. Emergency Room left us, he scribbled on a set of forms and handed them to me for check out.

Diagnosis: "Forehead laceration (commonly known as carpet burn) from impact."

I took my kid to the ER for a carpet burn.

> My first child shoved a raisin up her nose while sitting on my lap as we were watching a movie.
>
> She started freaking out and I tried everything to get it out!
>
> I ended up having to take her to the ER (where I WORK) to have it removed.
>
> Of course, it managed to swell from all the moisture in her nose to the point that she had to be sedated to get it out.
>
> Felt like mom of the year...and all of my co-workers had a good laugh, too.

> Had to call poison control because
> my one-year-old got caught eating
> her own poop.
>
> Her breath smelled terrible
> for the rest of the day.

Shit eating grin

MY KIDS WERE PLAYING IN THE YARD AND IT
BECAME TOO QUIET ALL OF THE SUDDEN.

UPON INVESTIGATION, I FOUND MY ONE-YEAR-OLD PLAYING
IN WHAT APPEARED TO BE A PUDDLE OF AC UNIT RUN-OFF
MIXED WITH SWALLOW DROPPINGS FROM THE TREES ABOVE.

WHEN HE TURNED TO ME, HIS FACE, HANDS AND MOUTH WERE
PLASTERED WITH A LITERAL SHIT EATING GRIN!

I IMMEDIATELY CALLED POISON CONTROL, BUT THEY SAID I
JUST HAD TO WAIT IT OUT AND WATCH FOR HALLUCINATIONS
OR VOMITING BEFORE BRINGING HIM IN.

THANKFULLY WE MADE IT OUT OF THIS ONE UNSCATHED.

@ferrise44

At least she's not pregnant...

WHEN MY DAUGHTER WAS THREE-YEARS-OLD, I CAME UPSTAIRS AFTER A LONG
NIGHT OF WORKING TO FIND HER FACE DOWN, ARMS AND LEGS ALL SPRAWLED
OUT ON MY BED (SHE NEVER SLEPT IN OUR BED).

I QUICKLY LOOKED DOWN AND SAW TINY FOILS AND MY BIRTH
CONTROL PILLS POPPED OUT ALL OVER THE FLOOR.

OF COURSE I THOUGHT SHE WAS DEAD FROM POISONING
AND SHOOK HER WHILE SCREAMING HER NAME IN TERROR.

ONCE I REALIZED SHE WAS ALIVE, I STARTED COUNTING HOW MANY PILLS WERE
LEFT (AFTER HUNTING FOR THEM EVERYWHERE), HOW MANY SHOULD HAVE
BEEN GONE AND DEDUCED THAT, AT MOST, SHE ATE TWO PILLS.

I CALLED POISON CONTROL TO EXPLAIN THE SITUATION AND WAS
ASSURED BY THE WOMAN ON THE LINE THAT IF SHE ONLY ATE
TWO PILLS, SHE WOULD BE FINE.

I EXPRESSED MY RELIEF AND THOUGHT (IN BAD JUDGEMENT) THAT THIS WOULD
BE A GOOD TIME FOR A JOKE TO LIGHTEN THE MOOD.

SO I SAID, "WELL AT LEAST WE KNOW SHE'S NOT PREGNANT!" I WAS SURE CPS
WOULD BE AT MY DOOR SHORTLY AFTER.

@mirandainclt

No blackberries

WHEN MY OLDEST DAUGHTER WAS TWO-YEARS-OLD, WE WENT OUT TO DINNER.

I BROUGHT ALONG SOME EXTRA FRUIT AND VEGGIES
TO KEEP HER ENTERTAINED.

ABOUT HALF WAY THROUGH THE MEAL SHE STOPPED EATING AND
WOULDN'T CLOSE HER MOUTH OR SWALLOW.

I FREAKED OUT THINKING SHE COULD HAVE SWALLOWED A BUTTON BATTERY
OR SOMETHING HORRID LIKE THAT SO WE RUSHED HER TO
URGENT CARE FOR CHEST X-RAYS.

WE SPENT HOURS THERE TRYING TO FIGURE OUT WHAT WAS WRONG.
SHE STILL WOULDN'T SWALLOW AND WAS DROOLING ALL OVER THE PLACE.

TURNS OUT SHE DIDN'T LIKE BLACKBERRIES THAT I HAD BROUGHT
FOR HER DINNER.

SHE HAD EATEN BLACKBERRIES BEFORE BUT APPARENTLY DECIDED MID DINNER
THAT THAT THEY WEREN'T FOR HER ANYMORE. SHE STILL WON'T EAT THEM
LIKE TWO YEARS LATER.

@Stephjowbaiz

UNSUSPECTING

BYSTANDERS

HAVE YOU OR SOMEONE YOU KNOW BEEN VICTIMIZED BY A TODDLER?

Are you a parent who has stood by, watching in horror as something down right terrible pops out of your toddler's mouth in front of an innocent stranger?

Don't worry, you are not alone.

We've all been there and lived to tell the tale.

— 66 —————

My son went through a stage of refusing to brush his teeth.
After begging and bribing I broke down and said,
"Well if you don't brush your teeth your going to get meth mouth."

I even showed him a picture of rotten teeth.

Well, off we went to the dentist, where we happened to get a new hygienist.

The hygienist asked my son if he brushed his teeth twice a day and he replied by saying,
"Yep, I sure don't want meth mouth!"

————————— 99 —

@ginnie.raines

Shopping at Harris Teeter in the baking section with three-year-old.
Greet the lady next to us with a smile. She smiles back.
Then three-year-old yells, "I don't like PENIS!!"
"What, Buddy?!?"
Again, but much louder, "I DON'T LIKE PENIS!!"
Stranger quickly turns her cart around and leaves without finding her items.
Turns out he was looking at pecans and saying, "I don't like peanuts."

@kendall.brooke.bing

My daughter has recently been naming all of her toys with a -y at the end of them
(giraffe-y, unicorn-y, banana-y). During her bath one night, she had an octopus toy.
Welp. She named it Octopussy and she hasn't stopped saying that name since.
While checking out at the grocery store she said to the grocery store employee,
"I have an octopussy at home!" I don't know who was more embarrassed, him or me.

@tadebra417

I walked into the liquor store with my three & six-year-olds.
My three-year-old asks, "What store is this?"
I ignore her because we are around quite a few people, but my six-year-old answers,
"The wine store." Then my three-year-old (loud as hell) says, "More wine?!"

@karly.rosetti

My oldest darling angel baby went through a phase where she would look every
older-looking human we encountered dead in the eye and say, "You old. You die soon."

@ashlynnward

After being asked if she's excited about having a new baby, my then
three-year-old daughter answers, "Ugh! My momma said she doesn't want anymore babies!
That baby isn't ours because it belongs to two guys!"
I was a surrogate.

@capt21011

Picture this...Mother standing in the quiet, but busy bank line, toddler playing at her feet.
Toddler hugs mom from behind; her nose ends up near mom's bottom.
Toddler says, "Ewwww! Mommy, your bottom stinks." There's no coming back from that one.

@smithie9484

At our aquarium, some poor young girl has the daunting task of sitting in a giant oyster
wearing a shimmering mermaid tail and seashell bra while kids pose with her for pictures.
My kid, who clearly inherited my social awkwardness, sits down and looks at the mermaid
tail pensively. Then she asks, "Where's your vagina? How do you go to the bathroom? Do
you have a hole in your butt?" I just. I died. Right there. I didn't even give the mermaid a
chance to respond. Just scooped my kid out of the oyster and avoided the exhibit all day.

@bethanyaven

We were traveling and attended a different church from our usual.
At the time, my two-year-old son pronounced "paci" as "p*ssy."
So, in the middle of a dead silent prayer, he yells,
"I WANT P*SSY!" at the top of his lungs. I wanted to die.

FRIENDLY

SKIES

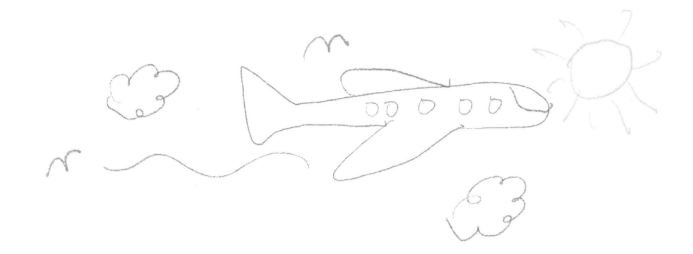

TRIGGER WARNING!

If you are sensitive, have anxiety or plan to fly with your toddler at any point,
I beg you not to read this chapter.

If you are any of those things (or a hot combo of all, like yours truly),
and still choose to keep reading, don't say I didn't warn you.

The 15 Terrible Things That Happened When I Flew Solo With My Toddler

1.

Upon entering security, my toddler fell suddenly and desperately in love with his stroller. As in, the moment he needed to get out of it to proceed through security, he absolutely could not part with his stroller. Heartbroken sobbing ensues.

2.

The TSA agent requested that my heartbroken, recently separated from his favorite stroller, twenty month old walk through the metal detector on his own. Towards a stranger and away from his beloved ~~mother~~ stroller.

3.

After picking up my sobbing toddler and carrying him through the metal detector, we then waited for my hands to be swabbed for bomb making residue. Obviously, they tested positive because I have a side gig as a bomb maker.[1]

4.

Upon testing positive for explosives, the process gets a little aggressive. Not to be outdone, my toddler saw a situation escalating and the attention moving away from him and decided to throw what can only be described as The Meltdown of The Century. For his first move, he threw himself onto the floor and cried so hard that he left an actual puddle of tears on the floor.

---

1   Although I'm sure it's obvious, for legal reasons I have to state that this is sarcasm.

5.

After begging the TSA agent who was unpacking and un-organizing every single one of
our bags to please do whatever he needed to do to return the stroller back to me,
I strapped the baby in, only for him to test the limits of the windbreaker fabric of the umbrella
stroller. I was so afraid he was going to flip himself backwards that I took him out.
He proceeded to flail around on the floor of security and somehow loosened his diaper.

6.

He then peed out of his diaper and soaked his pants and the floor of security.

7.

After our bags are searched, they are left open until two female TSA agents are
available to escort me, our bags and my still fully hysterical toddler into a small,
windowless room for a full body search.

8.

I was not allowed to remove anything from my bags until the search was complete,
so I had to strap the urine soaked baby back into the now hated umbrella stroller.
At this point, he is crying so hard he is choking, his screams are reverberating around the
windowless room and I was not allowed to go to him and hold him.

9.

As my boobs and top knot were getting a pat down, I began to cry.
Not because that was quite a bit of action for a toddler mom but because the
baby was still crying, the body search was going to take four total minutes and,
get this, our flight was due to take off in just 20 minutes at that point.

10.

After the search, I asked the two female TSA agents to just leave us in the room and shut the
door. I pulled the baby out of the urine soaked stroller and attempted to change his diaper while
we were both standing up. Because we were in a room meant to find drugs and/or bombs, there
were no trash cans, so I put the soaked diaper and pants in my purse. The screaming escalates
and so does my own crying.

11.

Once his clothes and diaper were changed, I attempted to soothe him, still shut in the bomb room, knowing there were hundreds of people listening to us lose our shit. I spent so many agonizing minutes trying to calm him and pack my bags at the same time, knowing the clock was ticking and I was dangerously close to missing my flight.

12.

I calmed him down somewhat and had no choice but to strap him back in his soaking wet stroller so that I could get us (and our crap) to the gate.
I managed to wrangle him in, open the door to the bomb room and meet the eyes of countless TSA agents who were just staring at us. Staring.

13.

We made our way to an elevator, which in my opinion, was a victory in and of itself, but had to stop as soon as we got out so that I could hold the baby. He was beyond upset. Nothing would calm him—food, drinks, Peppa, bribery fruit snacks, nothing. I gave up. I just stood in the middle of the Charlotte airport holding him, with all of our stuff dumped out around us. People stepped over us, a cart of supplies had to wait behind us, and I'm fairly certain someone snapped an iPhone pic of us as they walked by.

14.

After finding an acceptable bribery snack, taking off and then putting both shoes back on, and countless hugs and whispered pleas of "What do you need?!" I decided to try to make it to the gate, so I carried my 30lb toddler, drug my rolling suitcase and pushed the stroller as quickly as I could through the entire E concourse (50 something gates) and made it to the gate just in time to see the plane pull away from the jet bridge.

15.

We missed the flight.

In hindsight, I guess it could have been worse.

There could have been vagina talk...

> Luckily, this story is about the toddler sitting in the row behind us and not my own. The little boy behind us was going a teensy bit crazy while the other passengers were boarding so his mom says to him, "Come sit in my lap."
>
> The little boy then screams, loud enough for the whole plane to hear, "No mommy, your vagina smells!"
>
> I turned around and offered the mom a sympathetic smile before cracking up and counting my lucky stars that my own two-year-old was not the culprit.

> We were staying in downtown Charleston and my 18-month-old son was sleeping in the room so I was in the living room.
>
> I looked at the monitor and saw he was up and playing with something.
>
> He had gotten undressed and was squeezing the pee out of his diaper.
>
> When I walked back in the room, he was standing there peeing out of the corner of the pack 'n play.
>
> We will not be invited back there!

THE FIRST (AND ONLY) TIME WE FLEW WITH OUR SON WE KNEW SOMETHING WAS GOING TO HAPPEN BECAUSE HE'S FERAL.

HE DID OKAY ON THE WAY THERE, BUT AS WE WERE WAITING IN THE TSA LINE ON THE WAY BACK, HE WAITED UNTIL WE WERE NEXT IN LINE, DUCKED UNDER ALL THE ROPES AND JUST TOOK OFF.

OUT OF NOWHERE. NOT A SINGLE SIGN HE WAS ABOUT TO BOLT.

GROWN ADULTS MOVED OUT OF THE WAY FOR HIM, BUT NOBODY MOVED WHEN MY HUSBAND AND MOM TRIED TO GO AFTER HIM, SO HE GOT QUITE THE HEAD START.

MEANWHILE, I'M STANDING THERE WITH OUR BABY TRYING TO EXPLAIN TO A VERY UNAMUSED TSA AGENT WHAT WAS HAPPENING.

HE MADE IT ALL THE WAY TO THE BAGGAGE CLAIM AT THE SAN DIEGO AIRPORT.

MY HUSBAND HAD TO FULL ON SPRINT AFTER HIM WHILE MY MOM CORNERED HIM FROM THE OTHER DIRECTION.

HE WAS LAUGHING MANIACALLY WHEN ALL THREE WALKED BACK.

HONESTLY, IT'S A MIRACLE WE WERE ALLOWED ON OUR FLIGHT AND NOT INTERROGATED.

MORAL OF THE STORY:
ALWAYS LEASH YOUR TODDLER AND TRAVEL WITH A GRANDPARENT.

Always bring extra clothes

MY THREE-YEAR-OLD WAS DOING REALLY WELL POTTY TRAINING,
BUT I WASN'T SURE I TRUSTED HIS BLADDER ON AN AIRPLANE YET.

I DECIDED TO PUT HIM IN A PULL UP.

SINCE WE DID THE PULL UP, I DIDN'T BRING EXTRA SHORTS.

MY HUSBAND TOOK HIM TO THE RESTROOM DURING OUR LAYOVER
AND I GOT A PANICKED CALL FROM THE BATHROOM.

"DO WE HAVE ANY EXTRA CLOTHES IN THE CARRY ON?!?"

WELL, CRAP.

APPARENTLY, HE WASN'T USED TO HAVING PANTS ON WHEN HE SAT ON THE POT-
TY SO HE DIDN'T SPREAD HIS LEGS OR PUSH HIS PEEPEE DOWN AND PROCEEDED
TO PEE ON EVERYTHING—INCLUDING HIS PANTS AND MY HUSBANDS PANTS.

AFTER WALKING THE ENTIRE AIRPORT WITH A VERY UPSET
THREE-YEAR-OLD AND A SLEEPING ONE-YEAR-OLD, WE FOUND OUT THAT NOT
ONE STORE IN THE DALLAS LOVE AIRPORT CARRIED SHORTS.

MY POOR HUSBAND HAD TO HAND WASH HIS SHORTS
IN THE AIRPORT SINK AND DRY THEM UNDER THE HAND DRYER.

@trishavaiMarroque

Stinky feet

"

Flying with my two-year-old and she's sitting in the window seat.

She leans backward toward the seat behind her and loudly states, "Ewww stinky feet!"

The person behind us had their foot propped up on her armrest.

The worst part is that she "smells" things by putting them in her mouth.

My. Baby. Licked. A. Strangers. FOOT.

"

@kmmn22

What's wet?

First (and only) time flying alone with my one-year-old.

We get the seats in the first row of the plane to have extra room/some play space and I put him down on a blanket on the floor to play while I put the bag in the overhead.

When I sat down and picked him up, he was soaking.

I assumed he'd peed through his diaper, so I get our bag out of the overhead while holding said screaming toddler as people squeezed past, glaring, and changed him.

I then put him down on the floor on top of my sweater so I could put our bag back again.

When I picked him back up, he was soaked again.

Turns out the person sitting in our seats on the previous flight threw up all over the floor and my son and was actually covered in a stranger's watered-down, half cleaned up vomit.

We hadn't even taken off yet and every piece of our clothing, a blanket, and half of our toys were wet and contaminated.

They couldn't convince anyone to change seats with us.

Longest three hours of my life.

@kellylovesbaby

Roadie milk

ON OUR FIRST BIG ROAD TRIP WITH OUR JUST OVER
ONE-YEAR-OLD DAUGHTER, I DECIDED TO UTILIZE THE "FANCY" COOLER
IN OUR SUPER COOL NEW MINI VAN TO STORE HER "ROADIE" OF MILK.

UPON GETTING STUCK IN TRAFFIC AND HAVING A FUSSY BABY, I GAVE HER THE
MILK IN A DESPERATE ACT TO RESTORE THE PEACE.

UNFORTUNATELY I MUST HAVE ACCIDENTALLY TURNED THE
COOLER OFF AND I UNKNOWINGLY GAVE HER SOUR MILK!

SHE LET US KNOW ABOUT 10 MINUTES DOWN THE ROAD WHEN SHE VOMITED
CURDLED SOUR MILK ALL OVER OUR FANCY NEW MINI VAN.

@rooshrop

Sleepy throw-up

I TOOK A SOLO ROAD TRIP FROM SEATTLE TO SPOKANE
(ABOUT A FOUR HOUR TRIP) WITH MY ONE-YEAR-OLD.

ABOUT AN HOUR INTO THE TRIP HE THREW UP ALL
OVER HIMSELF AND HIS CAR SEAT.

BY THE TIME I MADE IT TO THE NEAREST REST STOP,
HE HAD FALLEN ASLEEP.

I DEBATED WITH MYSELF IF I SHOULD STOP AND WAKE HIM UP OR FORGE ON.
I DECIDED TO JUST GO FOR IT.

SO, FOR THREE HOURS I DROVE WITH MY PUKE-COVERED
BABE UNTIL WE GOT HOME.

NEEDLESS TO SAY, THOSE CLOTHES AND CAR SEAT GOT THROWN AWAY
AS SOON AS WE GOT HOME.

@melaniemcnaughten

INSULTS &

OTHER
ONE-LINERS

MY FIRST BORN HAS
TWO LOVE LANGUAGES:

Quality time and touch.

When I was pregnant with his sister, he and I were laying on the sofa, soaking in some down time, filling that love language cup of his when he rolled over and placed his tiny little toddler hand on my face.

I stared deep into his eyes, wondering how I had made such an incredible, loving little boy.

Then he began to count.

Loving and smart! What an amazing human I've brought into this world!

As he counted, his little hand turned from a loving caress to a pointing finger that landed one by one on the giant, angry pregnancy-induced zits on my face.

He counted and counted, practicing all of the numbers that Micky Mouse Clubhouse must have been teaching him.

And when he was done, he gently and sweetly said, "Mama! That's the most I counted! So many bumps on here!"

Motherhood is nothing if not humbling.

@ashjeanpitt

My daughter woke up last week and walked in on me in the closet getting dressed.
Before I realized, she says, "Woah, mama, your butt is way too big for those underwear!"
I respond with something like, "Give mama some privacy and don't look at it," to which she
nonchalantly replied, "Well it's pretty hard not to" as she walked out of the closet.

@jaymecrya_do

My three-year-old just last week announced,
"Mom, you have white hair, you can go to heaven now."
Thanks son, these grey hairs are from you!

@natNiepaige93

When my younger brother was a toddler, my mom was sitting at the table
looking over money stuff and she said, "Ugh, I hate budgeting."
He then shouts, "Stick to the budget bitch!" We didn't even know he knew that word!

@lammophyl

I'm not big on cooking but one night I went all out making dinner.
So, of course, my then three-year-old son refused to eat a bite.
He went outside to play while I cleaned up and after a few minutes he came back inside to
hand me a flower and told me, "I'm sorry... that you don't make better dinners."

@cme1515

I was chatting with my three-year-old about what princess she wanted
to be for Halloween when I said maybe I could be one too.
She looked me dead in the eye and said I could be Ursula because I look like her.

@stephjonbaie

My four-year-old and I we were showering together after a pool day.
I was seven or eight months pregnant.
She looked me up and down and said, "Why do your nipples look like that!?!"
with a horrified look on her face. I proceeded to explain that I would be making milk for her
baby sister when she was born. Cue horrified look.
Apparently she was glad her nipples didn't look like mine.

@abbymargaret

When my littlest brother was born my middle brother was three.
He walked in on my mom breastfeeding and stopped, look straight at her, and said
DOES DADDY KNOW WHAT YOU ARE DOING!?

@amnurst

While I was nine+ months pregnant, my personal grooming took a backseat.
While taking a shower with my toddler, he so kindly asked why I had a monkey in my butt.

@stacyrivas

My son was two and he was listing all the things he loved about me at bedtime.
"I love your nose." *Kisses my nose*
"I love your cheeks." *Kisses my cheeks*
"and I LOVE your mustache!" *Kisses my upper lip*
It goes without saying that shiz got waxed ASAP.

@icgordo

When our son was two-years-old we were playing with his trains.
He came over to me and said,
" Mommy, you have the best choo choo tracks!"
talking about the lines on my forehead...

ZOOM

THE YEAR 2020

brought us a new element of toddler parenting:
working virtually from home while parenting full-time.

And with that, came a new platform ripe for the toddler takedown:

Zoom

Whoever thought it was wise to bring your boss, clients, big-wigs and colleagues
into your home—live and on camera—clearly never parented.

> "So my husband's first ZOOM meeting with his new boss was a shit show.
>
> Our two-year-old decided to pick up our Frenchie and hand him to my husband during the call.
>
> Husband takes the dog.
>
> Toddler crawls into his lap as well.
>
> Dog barfs on toddler, toddler barfs on husband, husband barfs to the side....all on camera."

@marykimblackwell

Buzz cut

WHILE HUSBAND AND I WERE BOTH TIED UP ON CONFERENCE CALLS, OUR SON CAME UP NEXT TO US, GRINNING EAR TO EAR OVER THE HAIR CUT HE GAVE HIMSELF.

AND THE WORST PART WAS NEITHER OF US COULD EVEN REACT BECAUSE WE WERE BOTH IN LIVE VIDEO MEETINGS.

THE HAIR CUT WAS SO BAD THAT WE HAD TO BUZZ HIS HEAD.

BUT NOT UNTIL WE LET HIM SHOW OFF HIS DIY CUT FOR A FEW DAYS.

MY HUSBAND IS A FINANCIAL ADVISOR AND WAS ON A CALL
WITH A NEW CLIENT. HE WAS SPEAKING TO THEM WHEN MY
THREE-YEAR-OLD RAN OVER TO HIM YELLING,
"DADDY, DADDY, GET THIS OFF MY HANDS!" WHILE PROCEEDING TO
WIPE SOMETHING ONTO HIS HANDS.

IT WAS POOP.

SHE HAD JUST GONE TO THE BATHROOM, HAD A BAD WIPE,
AND GOT POOP ON HER HANDS. MY HUSBAND DIDN'T REALIZE
WHAT IT WAS UNTIL AFTER THE CALL!

HE ENDED UP FINALIZING THE DEAL WITH POOP ON HIS HANDS!

Poop paralysis

> Nothing like a toddler to humble you when
> you're feeling like a boss.
>
> Huge presentation time at work, face is on, hair is done,
> mama is ready to go!
>
> Ten minutes into my zoom call, I'm finding my groove, when my
> three-year-old slams open my office doors.
>
> Pants around his ankles, he shimmies his nekkid little butt next to
> me and screams, "Umma, Umma! I just pooped, wipe my butt!"
>
> Never have I ever shut my laptop screen so fast in my life.

@simplyeveryblog

Creeper

> My son just creeps in the back of my zoom meetings like a serial killer.

@Rachel.n.284

COOL MOM

SEEKS

COOL MOM SEEKS OPEN-MINDED, NON-HELECOPTER, COOL MOM FRIEND

I AM: a lover of yoga pants, enjoy hiding my lack of bra with a blanket scarf and never have clean floors.

I speak fluent sarcasm, Starbucks and wine and can enjoy all of the above morning, noon or night.

I am open to new adventures (but only if they occur before nap time) and used to be incredibly punctual.

I never answer the phone and sometimes respond to text messages in my head but I'm worth it, promise.

YOU ARE: nonjudgmental, open to allowing our children to "free play" in my gated play room, not opposed to purposefully avoiding Pinterest-y activities.

You are willing to ignore my dirty floors and open to feeding our toddlers processed foods.

You are available to get together at 9am on a week day to burn the hours until nap time.

You are also able to overlook the fact that I may not shower for days at a time.

Bonus points if you must drive past a Starbucks to get from my house to yours, if you have an inappropriate sense of humor and think your kid is sometimes kinda rogue.

Double bonus points if you own more than one brand of dry shampoo at all times, believe that a somewhat matching work out top and bottom is an outfit and expect a glass of wine during late afternoon play dates.

We both enjoy sitting down at the playground, commiserating over our shared exhaustion and trusting that our children will learn to play together without our constant, um, guidance.

Whistlers need not apply. [1]

---

1   If you got that Big Bang Theory reference, you're in.

SECRET'S

OUT

SOMEONE SHOULD REALLY INVENT A MODERN MOM'S SCRAPBOOK

You know, the type of scrapbook where you preserve the moments that are major markers in motherhood. And, no, I'm not talking about baby's first step.

I'm thinking more along the lines of documenting Baby's First Blow Out, complete with photo evidence.

Or, Biggest Meltdown, with the location and cause in bold letters.

And, of course, we would need an entire chapter dedicated to a well-known toddler developmental milestone:

Spilling secrets.

Imagine jotting these down for posterity:

Doctor dad

> I was stressed to the max thanks to a new baby and having to cut my maternity leave short.
>
> My husband agreed to watch the two-month-old and two-year-old so I could get a massage.
>
> Later that evening, my two-year-old says, "Baby hit her head. Her crying."
>
> My husband then confessed that our toddler pulled the baby from her swing and dropped her on the hardwood floor. SIX HOURS ago.
>
> "But she's fine. I googled it."
>
> Y'all. I'm a pediatrician.

@d_mcghee

@theheartcollective

We rolled into church barely on time one Sunday. The children's sermon that day happened to be on timeliness, and someone commented on his being late. Danny replied, "We would've been, but daddy and mommy showered together to save time."

@katiejlang

My SIL took her daughter to their third baby's eight-week appointment. Her daughter had EXPLICIT instructions not to tell anyone about the new baby until they announced. Guess who spilled the news the minute my MIL walked in the door later that day.

@kellytschida

When we were at Pizza Hut for lunch my husband kindly offered to take the kids to the bathroom. Pretty soon the three kids come out yelling that they had to leave because Dad was peeing out his butt and it stunk too bad for them to stay in there. Everyone heard and was laughing. My husband was NOT impressed.

@charlotteaanderstinj

My daughter used to walk around chanting *whoosh shloop whoosh sloop* and if anyone asked her what she was saying she would proudly tell them, "That's the sound my mommy's boobies make when they are getting sucked." I was exclusively pumping for my son. The amount of times I had to explain myself was mortifying.

@jennicohensur

While teaching preschool, we were discussing hobbies and all the kids were talking about what their families like to do. One girl said that her parents wrestle. And they "wrestle" without clothes on. It was hard to look at them when they picked her up from school.

@fMeighminning

Not my kids this time, but I worked the pre-k class at church and one of our sweet three-year-old girls was in there. We were using a pair of play handcuffs as an illustration and she yells out, "My mommy has some of those! They are pink and fuzzy and she keeps them by the bed!" Her mom was one of our worship leaders every Sunday.

@michelleatagu

My daughter actually spilled on my husband. He took her to the golf club and when they got back, she told me, "I saw daddy's friend who took all his money!"

@mfromille

When we were going through the adoption process,
my daughter's friend's mom was pregnant with twins.
The friend said, "My mommy is having TWO babies!"
To which my daughter replied, "Well, my mommy is BUYING two babies!"

POTTY

TRAINING

NATURALLY,

we couldn't write an entire book about toddlers and not include a chapter on potty training.

I do wish that I had some cute personal anecdote to share, or maybe some advice or well-wishes but I think we all know that's just not in the cards on this one.

I'll just say this and leave the rest for our Mom Conglomerate:

One of my children was potty trained within three days using only loving and encouraging reminders.

My other child was trained over a grueling four month period that ended only when the bribery stakes got high enough for her liking.

And in case you're wondering, neither situation brought out the best in me.

Poop-scrubber facial

> On the way to the potty my two and a half-year-old accidentally let out a turd on her bedroom floor. I scrubbed the floor with a brush and some cleaner, which I rinsed and left on her bedroom dresser in case of further accidents.
>
> Fast forward to nap time.
>
> I check the monitor and notice she's awake and out of bed. I start scrolling around the room only to spot her sitting on the floor by the door, softly caressing her face with the previously mentioned poop-scrubber brush.

@annamarie0615

MY TWO AND A HALF-YEAR-OLD HAD TO POOP, SO HE RAN TOWARDS THE
BATHROOM BUT HE DIDN'T MAKE IT IN TIME.

WHEN HE PULLED DOWN HIS PANTS, LITTLE POOP NUGGETS FELL ON THE FLOOR.

HE IS YELLING THAT HE HAD AN ACCIDENT, BUT THEN STARTS SAYING,
"NO! NO, DON'T DO THAT!"

I RUN IN TO FIND MY ONE-YEAR-OLD EATING HIS POOP OFF OF THE FLOOR.

> As most toddlers do, my girls LOVE to join me in the bathroom.
>
> We've also been working on naming male and female anatomy to explain why mommy and daddy pee differently.
>
> One day, as I was having my "morning pee," my two-year-old started asking questions for clarification.
>
> "Mommy, are you peein' out your penis?"
> "No, baby."
> "Are you peein' out your butt?"
> "No, baby."
> (Then I went to wipe)
> "Mommy, you're peein' out your mustache!"

@kristaghuber

Guacamole treat

> My mom and I decided to treat ourselves to a guacamole snack after pick up. We brought my two and a half-year-old potty training daughter with us. As they prepared our tableside guac—our mouths watering—my toddler managed to escape the table and move toward the table next to us. Our eyes must have been off of her for one second before the waiter came running over to us and loudly announced that the baby had an accident. *No big deal*, I think to myself. Well, it turned out she had pulled down her pants and poopped on the floor of the restaurant! All I had to pick it up with was a brand new monogrammed outfit that she was supposed to wear for a holiday. That was my mom's favorite restaurant and we haven't been back in nine months.

@foodymess

Venting

MINE PEED DOWN A VENT IN OUR HOUSE. TWICE.

REST

STOP

CONGRATS!

You survived potty training and are feeling confident enough to venture out into the real world.

May I suggest just a few things to bring with you:

TRAVEL POTTY
TRAVEL POTTY LINERS
FULL PACK OF WIPES
HAND SANITIZER
SPARE UNDIES
SPARE PANTS
SPARE SOCKS (YEP, IT WILL DRIP ALL THE WAY DOWN TO THE SOCKS)
BEACH TOWEL AS AN ABSORBENT CHANGING SURFACE
TRASH BAGS
POST IT NOTES (THOSE AUTO FLUSH SENSORS ARE SCARY)
SPARE CLOTHES FOR MOM
SMALL HAND TOWEL TO LINE CAR SEAT
A FEW GALLON SIZED ZIPLOC BAGS

Concerned this might border on toddler doomsday prepping?

Trust me, as the mom who has driven home covered in someone else's pee while my kid was naked and freezing cold, sitting in a urine-soaked car seat with teeny tiny underpants drying across the AC vents, you're gonna be glad you did.

Gotta go

My favorite story to tell goes a little like this:

One holiday, our family traveled to D.C. to tour the monuments.

My sister was in the middle of being potty trained and had to go to the bathroom.

There wasn't a restroom nearby so she peed in a cup in the back of our mini van and as my mom was passing it to the front for my dad to toss it out, he hit the cup on the steering wheel and the pee went all over him.

Thankfully he took one for the team and walked around covered in pee so we didn't miss our time slot for the scheduled tour of the Lincoln Monument.

@2bkid449

Mommy toddler potty

"

I was traveling solo with both my toddler and infant
when, of course, my toddler had to pee.

But, more importantly, I had to pee!

I didn't know how I would go holding a baby *while* keeping my
toddler from licking the floor of a public bathroom, so....

I went pee in a plastic potty in the front seat of our car in a bank parking lot.

"

@Summersantana

I didn't see buttholes!

66 ——————————————————

We are constantly battling our toddler boys not to look under public bathroom stalls.
One day, as I gently reminded my four-year-old not to peek, he yelled,
"Don't worry mom, I didn't see any buttholes!"

Laughter erupted from several stalls and I couldn't get them out of there fast enough.

—————————————————— 99

@lineflan

Writing on the wall

WHEN MY SON WAS JUST POTTY TRAINED ENOUGH FOR ME TO BE
CONFIDENT WITHOUT EXTRA CLOTHES IN MY PURSE,
WE WENT TO THE BEACH WITH MY PARENTS.

AFTERWARDS, WE WENT TO SMALL RESTAURANT AND I TOOK HIM TO THE
BATHROOM RIGHT AFTER ORDERING OUR FOOD. I THOUGHT I WAS BEING SO
SMART BECAUSE HE WOULDN'T HAVE TO GO WHEN THE FOOD CAME OUT.

WE GO IN AND HE SAYS IT'S JUST PEE, SO HE STANDS.

I STAND BEHIND HIM TO OVERSEE.

SUDDENLY, I FEEL SOMETHING BEING BLOWN AGAINST MY LEGS WITH FORCE.

IT WAS SHIT.

HE THOUGHT HE WAS FARTING AND SHOT SHIT EVERYWHERE. THE WALLS,
MY LEGS AND HIS CLOTHES.

EVERYTHING COVERED.

WE DIDN'T HAVE ANY EXTRA CLOTHES, SO I HAD TO SEND MY MOM TO THE
ONLY OPEN STORE AROUND—A DOLLAR GENERAL. I NEEDED SHORTS, HE NEEDED
UNDERWEAR AND PANTS.

THE KICKER WAS THAT SOMEONE ELSE WAS IN THE STALL BESIDE US. I
SCREAMED, "OH MY GOSH!" AND THEN HE SAID, "OH! I THOUGHT IT WAS A
FART MOMMY! I POOPED ON THE WALL!"

@alimaren04

NEVER

HAVE I EVER

THE PHRASE
NEVER HAVE I EVER

used to conjure up wild nights out, poor choices and a raging headache...

but these days, it makes me think of the things I never even dreamed I would say until I became a mom.

Recently, our toddler recovered from a pretty rough case of Hand, Foot and Mouth disease. In case you've never experienced HFM, it has a ton of gross symptoms and side effects, some of which only show up in rare cases.

Our case must have hit the jackpot because we were lucky enough to endure one of the unusual, and most disgusting, post HFM reaction: nail shedding.

That's right, her tiny little finger and toe nails peeled right off of her hands and feet, leaving a trail of nail pieces all over our house.

Which leads me to the words that I am still shocked ever came out of my mouth—my shining *Never Have I Ever dreamed I would say such a thing* moment:

"We don't put our finger nails on our dinner plate. Please pick them up and put them in the trash can."

There's really no coming back from that, is there?

@megan_is_hafflesuife

"Why is there cinnamon gum on your bum hole? We don't put gum on our bum hole."

@andeeljb

"Please don't tickle your feet with your cheese."

@katiemcrenshaw

"No, you will NOT grow a penis. Ever." *cries because she wants a penis*

@laurajayne23

"Stop painting your brother's bum hole with my pastry brush!"

@cfenn731

"Your brother's penis is not a toy."

@kia4812

"That's not a penis. It's a nipple."
*repeated over and over while two-year-old angrily
insists that his daddy has penises on his chest*

@leighanfimard

"We don't put our hands in the toilet while we are peeing."

@ashleybeatrice

"That woman doesn't want your hand down her shirt."

@juliebonottedimarco

"Yes, you'll probably have a hairy 'gina too."

@mama-to-my-biscuit

"We don't stick dinosaurs in our butt."

@robinsahinen

"Stop dragging your sister around by her diaper with that bungee cord!!"

@majohason15

"Don't stick the toothbrush in the toilet!"

@irishsk8r66

"Get off of the counter and put down that knife!"

@nani-love87

"Do not. Do NOT eat that googly eye off the floor!"

@itsalphabetsoup

"No, even when you grow big and strong you still won't be able to stand and pee like daddy."

@lindseymoore

"This is a pants *on* party!"

DUDE'S

DAY

I'M NOT ONE TO
LEAVE ANYONE OUT,

so we certainly can't overlook the contributions of our male parenting counterparts.

This chapter is inspired by a story about me when I was little that my dad, "Captain," loves to tell. After being left alone with me back in the early '80's, he called my mom out of a business meeting and demanded that she come home to help him with "a situation."

And what sort of situation was so overwhelming that he had to retreat and call in reinforcements?

While in my crib for a nap, I had taken off my dirty diaper and wiped the contents all over the walls, myself, and between the spindles of my prized, and quite ornate, Jenny Lind crib.

My father simply could not bring himself to cross the threshold of the nursery thanks to the smell, so he supervised me from the door while my mom made her way home to rescue him.

To her credit, she stripped out of her business suit, scrubbed me, the walls and the room, took a shower, put her suit back on and went back to her meeting.

Dad Days were short lived after that.

Forgetting baby

> Our first dinner out as a family of five.
>
> Dinner is done and the oldest girl has to use the bathroom.
>
> So I take the two girls and leave my husband to pay the bill and bring our one-week-old baby (no judging, he was the third!) to meet us at the car.
>
> Luckily, our paths crossed at the entrance to the restaurant.
>
> He holds the door open for us and I'm like, "Where is the baby?!"
>
> He's like, "OMG I forgot him."
>
> Thankfully the waitress was standing guard over our baby sleeping in his car seat.
>
> He's like, "I forgot! I mean, we haven't had him that long."
>
> He will never live that down!

Car fire

MY DAD TOOK MY SISTER AND I TO THE DOUGHNUT PLACE IN TOWN
WHEN WE WERE LIKE SEVEN AND FIVE.

HE TOLD US STAY IN THE CAR.

WHEN HE CAME OUT WITH DOUGHNUTS HE SAW US SITTING ON THE
SIDEWALK AND PROCEEDED TO FUSS AT US FOR GETTING OUT.

EVENTUALLY, HE NOTICED THAT THE REASON WE GOT OUT WAS THE
CAR WAS ON FIRE. ACTUAL FIRE.

OF COURSE, WHEN MOM FOUND OUT SHE BLAMED HIM FOR
ALMOST ROASTING US IN A CAR FIRE.

@hestrotman

Poopy paci

WHEN I WAS A KID, MY DAD USED TO PUT MY PACI IN HIS MOUTH TO
WIPE IT OFF IF I DROPPED IT. AFTER HE CLEANED IT, HE'D TURN
IT AROUND SO I COULD GRAB IT.

ONE TIME I WAS HOLDING MY PACI AND DECIDED TO THROW IT.

SOMEHOW KNOWING WHAT WAS ABOUT TO HAPPEN, HE CAUGHT IT MID-AIR.

SO PROUD, HE STUCK IT IN HIS MOUTH (ANYWAY) GOT
MORE THAN HE BARGAINED FOR.

I HAD POOPED IN MY DIAPER AND IT WAS COMING OUT THE EDGE OF MY DIAPER.

APPARENTLY AS I WAS WALKING WITH PACI IN HAND, I SWIPED
MY ARM BESIDE MY DIAPER AND SOME POOP GOT ON MY PACI.

HE IMMEDIATELY SPIT IT OUT AND STARTED GAGGING.

AFTER THAT INCIDENT HE ALWAYS CHECKED MY PACI BEFORE
PUTTING IT IN HIS MOUTH.

MY DAD LITERALLY TASTED POOP.

@melia.hammond

Dino band-aids

> My husband and I were sitting on the couch,
> when we heard a bang and my oldest start crying.
>
> He came running out to us on the couch holding a box of condoms.
>
> He had gone through my husbands night stand drawer to get
> "a dinosaur band-aid" for his boo boo.
>
> Flash forward a few weeks later, my husband and son are at
> Target cashing out and my son noticed the guy behind them
> in line was also buying "dinosaur band-aids" and proceeded to
> yell at my husband, "Hey dad, he's buying Dino band-aids too!!!!"

@ourtiny_nest

"

When I was six-years-old, my mom left me alone with my dad
for the first time for an extended period of time.

She was going on a girls trip to Cancun and I was DEVASTATED.

I don't know why, but I was so distraught over her leaving us.

We had just had a huge snow storm in our town. Afte she left, and the sun had gone down,
I put on my snow suit, went outside, and wrote "GOD HELP ME" in giant letters across the
front embankment of our yard—truly large enough so they could see it from space.

My dad called my mom and was like,
"You will never guess what your daughter just wrote in the snow across our lawn...."

"

Frozen jeans

THIS STORY IS ABOUT MY DAD!

IT WAS FEBRUARY IN MINNESOTA AND MY MOM LEFT MY DAD ALONE
WITH MY SISTER WHO WAS TWO AND A HALF-YEARS-OLD.

SHE SHIT HERSELF BAD—ALL OVER HER JEANS.

INSTEAD OF WASHING THE JEANS, POPS JUST THREW
THEM OUT IN THE WOODS TO HIDE THE EVIDENCE.

MOM GOT HOME AND ASKED HOW EVERYTHING WENT.

"OH GREAT! NO ACCIDENTS!"

MOM ASKED IF HE WAS SURE ABOUT THAT AND, AS HE TURNED AROUND, HE
SAW MY MOM HOLDING UP A FROZEN PAIR OF SHITTY PANTS. OUR LABRADOR
RETRIEVED THEM FROM THE WOODS JUST AFTER MOM GOT HOME.

R-rated

MY HUSBAND ACCIDENTALLY TOOK OUR TODDLER TO
THE R-RATED MOVIE "HAPPY TIME MURDERS."

I LITERALLY DO NOT UNDERSTAND HOW IT HAPPENED.
MAYBE HE SAW JIM HENSON AND OVERLOOKED THE RATING
(AND TITLE I GUESS?).

AFTER A VERY INAPPROPRIATE OPENING SCENE, HE DRAGGED
OUR DAUGHTER OUT AS SHE WAILED,
"NOOOO! WHY CAN'T WE STAY FOR THE MOVIE"?

I CAN'T EVEN IMAGINE WHAT THE MOVIE STAFF AND AND OTHER PATRONS
THOUGHT AS HE WALKED INTO THE THEATER WITH HER.

@brittney_ac

THE

END

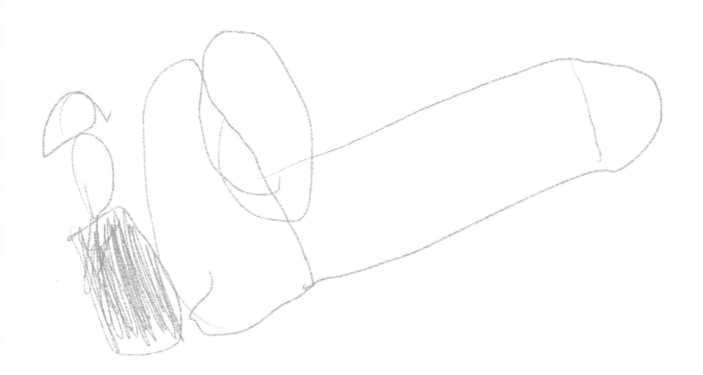

FRIENDS, WE'VE COME TO THE END OF OUR JOURNEY.

IT'S BEEN A WILD RIDE, BUT MOTHERHOOD IS NOTHING LESS.

IF I'VE LEARNED ONE THING IN ALL OF MY YEARS PARENTING,
HOSTING #TODDLERTUESDAY AND SHARING OUR STORIES, IT'S THIS:

At the very least, we can laugh about it.

THANK
YOU

Thank you to the hundreds of parents, grandparents and toddler adjacent individuals who tossed aside their dignity to share tales from the front lines of toddlerhood.

We are collectively grateful for your sacrifice.

CPSIA information can be obtained
at www.ICGtesting.com
Printed in the USA
LVHW071249240621
691054LV00005B/16

9 781955 077064